The Moment Before
the Music Begins

A T.E.A.M.™ Approach to Song Study

Lisa Campbell Albert
& Bill Lynch

The Moment Before
the Music Begins

A T.E.A.M.™ Approach to Song Study

Foreword by Taylor Louderman

VITA HISTRIA

Vita Histria

Las Vegas ◊ Chicago ◊ Palm Beach

Published in the United States of America by
Histria Books, a division of Histria LLC
7181 N. Hualapai Way, Suite 130-86
Las Vegas, NV 89166 USA
HistriaBooks.com

Vita Histria is an imprint of Histria Books. Titles published under the imprints of Histria Books are distributed worldwide.

Library of Congress Control Number: 2022938618

ISBN 978-1-59211-166-4 (softbound)
ISBN 978-1-59211-222-7 (eBook)

Contents

To all the students at Webster
University Conservatory of Theatre Arts
that challenged us to be specific in
articulating our approach to making
musical theatre more real and relevant
in their world.

Acknowledgement

If we attempted to list all of the people who have profoundly influenced us personally and professionally, we fear this section may be longer than the book you are about to read!

Friends, colleagues, mentors, you know who you are. We hope you see the influences you all have had on us in the following pages.

Foreword by Taylor Louderman

I've known Lisa Campbell Albert since I was in High School, which was many "one acts" ago; in fact, she is the co-developer and refiner of my vocal storytelling ability. Despite deserving every bit of pay for individualized coaching, she knew I drove over an hour to spend those ever-so essential moments with her gifts. Honorably, she chose not to charge me the full extent of what she deserved: a testament to not only her kindness but also her commitment to growing young talent and growing me. Following, she and I began a journey in a theatrical a cappella group: she as the director and me as a student. Her high expectations and extraordinary ability to lead challenged me in all the right ways. In addition, Lisa guided me through the process of application of acceptance into a dream school: The University of Michigan. In those times before, in between, and after, she coached me to belt, mix, and soprano my way to a competitive edge; in other words, you name it, she taught me: she pushed me, challenged me and ultimately tuned my ears and voice to the sounds of musical storytelling.

It was this intuitive coaching which sustained me through eight Broadway shows a week; MEAN GIRLS, KINKY BOOTS, and BRING IT ON on Broadway, all of which showcased her storytelling techniques through the voices of characters who borrowed them. Remarkably, Lisa never fueled my ego, but instead, gave me enough confidence to move forward; And, to this day, she refuses to claim her mark in my success. She may not know this, but it is my honor to coach alongside her. As for the students I pass along, I say this: I confidently pass them to a mentor with a gift (a secret of sorts). I know these students are in for lessons beyond "sounds of music." I believe once her gift is shared with them, like mine, their stories inevitably change, both in voice and in life.

The art of storytelling does not come with a "one-size fits all playbook" and yet, this book manages to erect clear guideposts encouraging artists to execute bold, honest choices while intentionally balancing audience and industry expectations. It is here, Lisa and Bill become storytellers of a slightly different sort, as their experiences intersect to share with readers a rare 360° view of this complex craft. One of my favorite highlights of the many woven within is their emphasis on working a process for not only those crafting the context but also the artist as a person; it is through this celebration of individualization that both authors announce the necessity to acknowledge that artistry comes from the artist. Indeed, it is too easy to "show up" in this career for others or for the next job; And, yet, I have found the same truth as Lisa and Bill; when I give myself permission to recognize my person and harness my person's "why," there is noticeably greater impact on an audience, scene partners, and the like.

So, admirably, together, Lisa and Bill speak a powerful truth and tell a story that vocalizes not only the artist as a character but also the artist as a person, two essential but often overlooked elements. On a personal note, still to this day, I am learning and often humbly celebrate lightbulb moments when in their presence; this book now defines one of those powerful moments. Indeed, Lisa and Bill are what you call "experts" in the business of musical storytelling. Each has invested well-beyond ten thousand hours supporting and coaching professionals and students. It is extraordinary to experience this duo working in tandem, blending their unique tools into one; this book is the result of a powerful collaboration that narrates a story of some extraordinary things, many of which are worth singing about.

Taylor Louderman

Introduction

Many of us love to think of ourselves as "theatre artists." We will maintain in our T.E.A.M. approach that before one can truly become an artist, one must become an expert practitioner of the craft. This opinion is supported by many others, in many other fields that may be considered "art." To quote the late, great Anthony Bourdain:

"Cooking is a craft, I like to think, and a good cook is a craftsman—not an artist. There's nothing wrong with that: The great cathedrals of Europe were built by craftsmen—though not designed by them. Practicing your craft in expert fashion is noble, honorable, and satisfying."

Anthony Bourdain, Kitchen Confidential: Adventures in the Culinary Underbelly, 2000

As Anthony Bourdain also demonstrated in his life and in his work, the application of craft to product is ultimately an expression of the culture that created that product.

We agree with Mr. Bourdain.

We maintain that the application of the craft of Musical Theatre has all too frequently become overshadowed by the desire to create the product of Musical Theatre. Since most of the genre is aimed at a commercial audience, and therefore aimed at returning yield on investment, it is understandable that the focus on product over process has exerted a compelling, perhaps dominant, influence upon modern Musical Theatre productions. This in turn has influenced the training of people seeking work in the modern Musical Theatre business.

However, we maintain that craft versus product is not mutually exclusive. In fact, we will argue in our T.E.A.M. approach that they are dependent upon one another if one is to elevate our craft to art.

Notice our attention to craft and art, not securing employment. There are some books specifically aimed at the audition process itself. This is not one of those books. This book focuses on the work required BEFORE you audition.

Some may read this book and feel it a bit "basic". However, no matter where you may be in your career, we feel we could all benefit from remembering WHY we sing beyond "We sing for our supper."

So to be explicit, we have no desire to offer our T.E.A.M. approach with the promise that if you apply our process you will book more gigs.

Still reading?

Here is what we will promise.

When you get booked, your experience will be richer.

Our T.E.A.M. approach offers a process focused on craft as a means of not just creating product, but of creating meaningful, authentic product. We firmly believe that the product of such craft is actually more commercially viable. After all, if one has little control over the process, how can one expect to have control over the product?

In our T.E.A.M. approach we will offer a process. We do not maintain it is the only process. Or that it is an all-encompassing process. However, it is a process we have developed over our combined years (more than we are willing to disclose) of personal and professional work experiences in Musical Theatre, conversations with our colleagues who continue to work in and create professional Musical Theatre, and years of training our future Musical Theatre colleagues. We will encourage you to use this as a starting point to develop your own process, and we will look forward to hearing your feedback. That is largely how we got to the point of writing this in the first place!

We could boast about the number of those who we have trained who are surviving, or even thriving, in professional Musical Theatre throughout the world. But this is not about us. It's about you. It's about inviting you to join us in our desire to create meaningful, impactful, truthful Musical Theatre.

To reiterate, Mr. Bourdain said:

"Practicing your craft in expert fashion is noble, honorable, and satisfying."

We offer this to you to do just that.

Lisa & Bill

Chapter 1
Nobody suddenly breaks into song and dance IRL! Right?

So what's the rap about Musical Theatre? Typically, people say nobody acts that way in real life. But is that true?

Our acting training was aimed at helping us understand how to behave truthfully under imaginary circumstances. But is singing and dancing truthful?

We will make the case it is, when applied correctly.

When people discuss the plays of Anton Chekov or Henrik Ibsen, yes, they seem realistic. But do people really talk like that? No! It is "real life" more highly organized. "Realism" allows the characters to be more articulate in moments of passion than any of us would likely be able to do under those circumstances. Don't we wish we could be that articulate in our most intense moments? Those moments are carefully shaped by the playwright. In dramas we recognize that while most people may not speak that well in moments of high stakes (IRL) we all wish to believe we could. In comedies we recognize we may not be that witty in moments of high stakes (IRL) but we all wish we could. Theatrical dialogue more closely resembles what we wish we would have said in the moment, as opposed to what we probably would say in the moment. We enjoy living vicariously through those characters and those moments.

Willing suspension of disbelief is the foundational contract between theatre artists and our audiences in general. However, we seem to apply it differently to what we consider "realism" and other "isms." After all, when someone dies in a "realistic" play, we accept it as true in the moment, but expect to see them at curtain call, don't we?

That's what an audience wants to experience — that moment when they could do that perfect thing in that perfect moment, but be able to go home safely and a bit wiser for the journey.

We seem to accept these aesthetics for realism, classic or contemporary, but what about other "isms?" So what about Shakespeare? Why do we treasure Shakespeare as "real?"

When people talk about Shakespeare, and why the characters speak in verse, a common response is when mere prose is not sufficient, characters require verse to constrain the breadth of human emotion.

What theatre artists do is organize real human impulses into an aesthetically presentable product, regardless of style. Shakespeare survives not only because of the history of kings and queens, but because Shakespeare captured the experiences of multiple strata of society. He also knew he needed to make a profit (the origin of commercial theatre). We are convinced if he were alive today, he'd be writing musicals.

So back to the premise: no one IRL breaks into song and dance, right? So Musical Theatre has to be just fake. Right?

Wrong.

Musical Theatre is founded upon the same real, human impulses as any other theatrical endeavor, but heightened. We maintain when mere verse is not sufficient, characters require verse and song.

We could cite many examples, but I (Bill) will offer this specific personal case study.

I went to a local pub in St. Louis in 2016, between lunch and dinner, intentionally to have a quiet meal and a pint. While I was aware that the 2016 Olympics were underway, I did not anticipate what I would encounter. It turned out that members of the Washington University of St. Louis track team were in the pub to watch the men's 1500-meter race.

This race typically takes approximately four minutes. From the gun, these guys were totally into it. Like any other distance sport, it takes a while for things to develop. However as the race developed it became clear that an American runner, Matthew Centrowitz, was in contention. My college "friends" were totally engaged. As the race evolved, they started yelling at the television to cheer, encourage, will Matthew on to victory. The closer he came to the finish, the more they yelled, jumped and pounded their fists on the bar and their feet on the beer-soaked floor. The closer he came to the finish, the more animated my college friends became.

As the race was coming to the end they were jumping up and down, screaming "Go Matthew, Go Matthew!" As he crossed the line victorious, they leapt in joy and embraced one another as they screamed. Then a truly unexpected thing happened: they spontaneously began singing the National Anthem of the United States in unison.

Isn't that the true IRL impulse for song and dance? Haven't all of you seen or experienced those moments? At a sporting event? After acing an exam? Running out of a class and railing at the professor who was so clearly out of touch? Jumping, screaming, with emotion mere words could not express?

That is the impulse for Musical Theatre! All we do, like Chekov, Ibsen, and Shakespeare, is take the real, human impulse, and then shape it into an aesthetic form that allows the audience to experience it vicariously.

That is what our T.E.A.M. approach seeks to shape.

Chapter 2
How the Music Talks to the Lyric

So… what is this T.E.A.M. approach that you speak of? What is its purpose? Where does it come from? Why should I apply it to my work?

All legitimate questions. I (Lisa) specifically remember talking with a student after a song study class and being asked, "We have all these specific rules and lists that we are expected to apply to our scenes and monologues. Why isn't there a checklist like that for analyzing a song?"

That is the reason for our T.E.A.M. approach.

After that conversation, I immediately thought it necessary to come up with something that would be easy to remember and easy to apply.

Just like sports teammates rely on each other to successfully achieve the goal of winning, so does a song rely on its T.E.A.M.-mates to achieve the winning goal.

What is winning in song study?

We define winning as truthfully pursuing an objective in a moment-to-moment way throughout the song. This includes the moment before the music begins and extends beyond when the music ends.

We truly believe that we sing better when we act better! By applying concepts we use as actors, we can take a step back as singers and rely on the technique to do the work. Now, technique is of the utmost importance in singing efficiently and correctly but it needs to be organic and trusted. In that way, we can put the focus on the acting moment and not on the singing moment. Our T.E.A.M. approach will not necessarily make you a better singer technically, but it will make you approach the music in a more specific way to engage your vocal technique to its fullest. It will make you understand how the music and lyrics are acting partners.

Something to remember is that everything you need to know about the song and who is singing it is IN THE MUSIC! There is no need to try and add something that isn't there; just find the truth in what already exists on the page. As David Mamet writes:

"Invent nothing, deny nothing."[1]

T.E.A.M. broken down looks like this:

T – *Tonal Color*

E – *Energy/Emotion*

A – *Accompaniment*

M – *Melody Line*

---

[1]David Mamet, *True and False: Heresy and Common Sense for the Actor*, 1997.

The specific definitions and how to apply the T.E.A.M. acronym will be outlined in Chapter 5.

Chapter 3
How the Lyric Talks to the Music

Obviously, we need lyrics to make a song. However, as noted in our previous chapter, our students tell us they have "all these specific rules and lists that they are expected to apply to their scenes and monologues". So we created a series of questions students should ask at the beginning of not just learning a song, but how to make that song THEIR song.

These questions start broadly; however, the more you drill down, the better. Start with what is explicit in the text but be ready to fill in the blanks with additional research and imagination based upon the text.

We call these questions the 9 Ws:

1.   Who?

2.   When?

3.   Where?

4.   Whom?

5.   What #1?

6.   What #2?

7.   What #3?

8.   What #4?

9.   Why?

The specific definitions and how to apply the 9 Ws will be outlined in the following chapter.

Chapter 4
Warming Up the T.E.A.M.

While there is no right or wrong in which questions you engage first, we believe that exploring the 9 Ws is a way to warm yourself up to maximize the benefit of our T.E.A.M. approach. We believe this because having a more complete understanding of the play will help you have a more specific understanding of the song in the context of the play.

As with our T.E.A.M. approach, students at times don't know what questions to ask at the beginning of not just learning a song, but how to make that song their song. So creating the 9 Ws is a way of creating a series of questions to initiate that process. These questions start broadly, however, the more you drill down, the better. Start with what is explicit in the text, but be ready to fill in the blanks with imagination based upon the facts found in the text.

The first step is to read the play beginning to end in one sitting. Read all of the author's notes, the stage directions, and the dialogue. When reading the lyrics try to read them as text, without thinking of how they may be sung. Try not to think of the answers to the questions below, rather experience the play. Once you have done this, put the play away for a day. Let the play live with you for a while...

Then re-read the play and make notes that will help you find exciting answers to the questions below. Assume that all choices in the play were made intentionally, even the names of the characters. When appropriate these questions should be answered in the first person. Also know that answers to one question may inform or change other answers as you continue. Sometimes the authors are explicit in providing the answers below.

Sometimes the answers are implicit. It is your job to determine what those answers will be. It will also be your job to use your imagination to fill in what the playwright has not provided.

1.   WHO?: Who are you?

What does the playwright specifically say about the character?

Character's name, age, relationship status, family, social status, ethnicity, gender identification, career, previous life events, life events that take place during the course of the play, world views.

Why are these important?

Someone who is 18 years of age is likely to have very different perspectives than someone who is 48. Someone who has a graduate degree might have very different perspectives than someone who completed high school.

This information may shape some of the answers to follow.

2. WHERE?: Where do the events take place?

Some plays are very specific about where the play takes place. For example, *In the Heights* takes place in the largely Hispanic-American neighborhood of Washington Heights in New York City. Some plays are less specific but provide important clues.

For example, in *Baby*, we know the play takes place on a college campus. We also find in the author's notes that the college campus is in New England. With a little more exploration we could choose a specific college that might help us form a mental picture of the campus.

3. WHEN?: When do the events take place?

Some plays are very specific about the year that the play takes place. For example, if the playwright says this is set in 1945, it's 1945!

Some plays do not specifically tell us what year the events take place. We may know when the play was copywritten or if it has been revised since its original publication. So the decision of what year it takes place will need to be made for a production, or for you if the song is being performed outside of a production.

For example, if in your "Who" you determined your character was gay there will be a very different environment if the play took place now or in 1970. If in your "Who" you determined your character was a BIPOC[2] female the same would apply.

In addition to the year, what time of year? What time of day? A play that takes place in a Michigan winter has a very different feel

---

[2] BIPOC is an acronym for Black, Indigenous and People of Color.

than a play that takes place in an Arizona summer. A song sung at sunrise has a very different feel than a song sung at sunset.

So when you have determined the "Where" and the "When" you have created the environment in which your character (the "Who") lives.

4. WHOM?: To whom are you speaking? Who is this person in relation to you?

This is always explicit in the text. However, more specificity will create a more personal connection to the lyric. For example, the text says you are singing to your teacher. Is that enough? Think of the different teachers you have had in your life. While the power dynamic of teacher/student remains constant, weren't your individual interactions different with different teachers?

Many times in musicals a song is a solo. But there still must be a "Whom" or there is no reason to sing. So here we must determine to whom are we singing. There are really two options: to the audience or to yourself.

If you are singing to the audience, who is that audience? Are they your friends? Are they your enemies? Are they people you are trying to enlist as allies?

In many songs, the character is "singing to themselves". But why would they need to sing out loud? IRL, when do we speak to ourselves out loud? When we have an internal dilemma that we must solve, we work through that problem out loud. The classic theatre example is the "To be or not to be" soliloquy. Hamlet is literally trying to decide whether it is better to be alive or dead. So he juxtaposes the pros and cons of both sides out loud so he can clearly see the two options before him and choose one.

5. WHAT #1?: What has happened before the play begins?

Remember, your character had a life before the events of the play. There will be clues in the four previous questions that will help you outline the critical events that shaped you prior to the beginning of the play.

6. WHAT #2?: What do you need?

You must define specifically what you need from the person to whom you are singing. It is also very helpful if you can answer the question "How will I know if I get it?"

7. WHAT #3?: What are you willing to do to get what you need from the other?

This starts easily — ANYTHING! However here we employ the classic "less is more" adage — do no more than is required, no less than is necessary. You know what you need, your partner will inform what you choose to do to get what you need, and when you need to change tactics.

8.   WHAT #4?: What is the immediate moment before?

To determine this, map out the events that have taken place since the play began. Determine what changes your character has experienced. Most importantly and specifically, determine what immediate event triggers the moment before the music begins.

9.   WHY?: Why MUST YOU SING?

In Chapter 1 we argued that the impulse for song and dance IRL is only at peak moments of emotional experience. Therefore, we must create the stakes that require verse and song to solve the immediate issue confronting us. We must be able to place ourselves in the imaginary circumstances we have created with the answers to the previous eight questions. This frees us to behave truthfully in the imaginary circumstances.

Putting all of the above together is how we make the song uniquely our own. It allows us to answer the essential question "What would *I* do in this moment?"

Chapter 5
T.E.A.M. Workout

A quick reminder, T.E.A.M. broken down looks like this:

T- Tonal Color

E — Energy/Emotion

A — Accompaniment

M — Melody Line

Let's take a look at the individual T.E.A.M. members and discuss how to use each.

T — Tonal Color

We use this term to describe what vocal quality best suits the song being explored. It could be a high, operatic voice for a song such as "Till There Was You" (as sung by Barbara Cook in *The Music Man*), a smoother, silkier sound for a jazz standard like "Save Your Love For Me" (as sung by Nancy Wilson), a mixed-belt sound for "I Wanna Dance With Somebody" (as sung by Whitney Houston), or it could be a full-throated, chest voice sound for "Everything's Coming Up Roses" (as sung by Ethel Merman in *Gypsy*). Imagine using that full chest "belt" on "Till There Was You", or how about a nice legit soprano singing Whitney's "I Wanna Dance With Somebody".

Doesn't REALLY seem right, does it?

So how do you discover the correct choice?

Ask these questions:

1.   What is the age of the character singing the song?

As we discovered in the first of the 9 Ws, age informs our vocal quality. Think of your own voice at the age of 8, at 18, at 28, and so on. Your life experiences also inform your vocal qualities. Working for years in a factory may have a different vocal impact than working for years in a library.

Before we continue with the next questions, let's clarify the difference between an up-tempo song, patter song, and ballad as seen in the *Merriam-Webster Dictionary*:

• An up-tempo song has a fast -moving tempo.

• A patter song uses lyrics in a rapid or mechanical manner for humorous effect.

• A ballad is a slow, romantic or sentimental song

On to the following questions.

2. Is the song energetic, needing a more percussive articulated approach in delivery as in an up-tempo song or patter song?

Many contemporary musical theatre, pop, and rock songs have a driving energy. Using a more chest oriented or mix-belt sound would give the lyric more punch and percussiveness achieving the drive needed.

3. Is the song more luxurious and smoother in sound, such as in a ballad?

Ballads written between 1940-1970 provide some classic examples, however there are many wonderful ballads written within the last 30 years that can live in this category as well. The artistry in ballads is found in the smooth, flowing musical phrases. Using a more head voice-oriented sound would allow these phrases to have more breadth, creating a warmer tone and, more than likely, a deeper sense of emotion. That's not to say that a chestier tone can't achieve the same effect, but a chestier tone is a bit more rigid and brassy than a more engaged head voice tone.

E — Energy/Emotion

The energy/emotion comes from the rhythm and dynamics of the song.

When we listen to music, one of the first things we recognize is the rhythm of the piece and how it makes us feel or even move. This is apparent when you see people tap their foot, slightly sway, or even bob their heads when listening to music. This is because rhythm affects us internally — our heart rate actually syncs up with rhythms. So depending on the tempo of the piece, our heart rate will adjust to that particular pulse.

How does that help us with our song?

Ask these questions:

1. Has the composer indicated tempo markings at the beginning and throughout the song?

At the beginning of most songs you will find a word or phrase (tempo marking) describing the pace and mood of the song. This is your first clue to the song's energy/emotion. For example, the tempo marking for "Let It Go" from *Frozen* by Anderson-Lopez and Lopez is "Halftime feel, Mysterious". Another example is "The Proposal" from *Titanic* by Maury Yeston. This tempo marking is "Brooding".

2.   Is there a lot of syncopation? (placement of rhythmic stresses or accents where they wouldn't normally occur)

Syncopation creates tension. Tension creates uneasiness — not necessarily good or bad, just feeling unsettled. Identifying this in the song can help us work to resolve the uneasiness we are experiencing. In "Fascinating Rhythm" by George and Ira Gershwin, the pulse of the song appears in unexpected places. Since we expect that pulse in traditional places, this creates anticipation and excitement. After all, It is called "Fascinating Rhythm"!

3.   Is there a lot of dynamic range? (loud or soft)

Dynamics can affect our emotion. For example, loudness can create excitement or power while softness can create calmness or sadness. Softness might also include intimacy while loudness might embrace a larger group. A song like "Seventy-Six Trombones" from Meredith Wilson's *The Music Man* uses volume to stir enthusiasm among the towns-folk.

4.   What kind of notes are being used? Are they rapid (8th and 16th notes) or are they slow (quarter/half/whole notes)?

You don't necessarily have to be able to read music to be able to identify what these notes look like. It's like reading a map. Every map has a legend that uses symbols to help interpret the map. Some of the symbols in the musical map are notes. Look at the examples below:

o — Whole note

♩ — Half note

♪ — Quarter note

♪ — Eighth note

♪ — Sixteenth note

You can see how the appearance changes as the notes divide in half. You can also see how the whole note has no "stem" and how the eighth and sixteenth notes add "flags" to the stem. As you add stems, the notes get faster; as you add flags, the notes get faster still. So just by identifying what the notes LOOK like you can discover what the music is doing. More whole notes will probably lean toward a slower song (ballad) while a song with lots of "stems and flags" will probably lean toward a faster song (up tempo, patter).

5.   Are the musical phrases long or short?

This question is interesting because ballads, up tempo and patter songs can use long phrases and short phrases. In a patter song such as "Getting Married Today" from Sondheim's *Company*, Amy sings in long frantic phrases due to a pre-marital panic attack. Short phrases in a ballad can be used to portray the character as having to take time to think of what needs to be said next. At the start of "Simple Little Things" from Schmidt and Jones' *110 in the Shade*, Lizzie's thoughts are segmented as she tries to articulate for the first time what she specifically wants in a relationship.

The length of the phrase indicates the length of the unit of thought as well as the urgency needed to say what needs to be said.

A — Accompaniment

The purpose of any sort of "team" is to come together in a unified effort to achieve a common goal. In volleyball the Setter assists the Hitter; in football, the Center helps the Quarterback; in business, the CFO supports the CEO; in theatre, the Actor listening responds to the Actor speaking. Working as a "team" yields a more productive result.

Same applies to a song.

It is very important, when analyzing the accompaniment, to listen to the song as a whole. Here's what was explained in Chapter 3: "The first step is to read the play beginning to end in one sitting. Read all of the author's notes, the stage directions, and the dialogue. When reading the lyrics try to read them as text, without thinking of how they may be sung. Try not to think of the answers to the questions below, rather experience the play. Once you have done this, put the play away for a day. Let the play live with you for a while…"

You should take this same approach with listening to your song of choice. So, let's change some of the words to make more sense regarding the song:

"The first step is to LISTEN to the SONG beginning to end in one sitting. Read all of the LYRICS WHILE LISTENING — DO NOT SING THEM. Try not to think of the answers to the questions below, rather experience the SONG. Once you have done this, put the SONG RECORDING away for a day. Let the SONG live with you for a while…"

Doing this exercise allows you to hear the song completely and experience the song from an external rather than an internal perspective.

Now it's time to locate the teammates in the accompaniment.

Ask these questions:

1.   Do the lyrics, melody, and accompaniment seem the same?

When we listen to a song, it is fascinating how the lyrics we hear align with the music that we hear. Sometimes lyrics and melody blend fluidly with the accompaniment, making the song feel seamless between the two. As an example, in "How Could I Ever Know" from *The Secret Garden* by Norman and Simon, the lyrics, accompaniment, and melody ebb and flow as a unit. When the lyrics reach the highest emotional peak so does the accompaniment and melody — all three elements working together in unison.

2.   Do the lyrics and melody seem different than the accompaniment?

Sometimes the lyrics and melody are in opposition with the accompaniment. In "Something's Coming" from Bernstein and Sondheim's *West Side Story*, Tony sings about the feeling he has that something of importance lies ahead. He sings in long, legato phrases while the accompaniment surges with syncopated energy. The juxtaposition of smooth to syncopated builds the sense of excitement for what is to be.

3.   Are the melody and accompaniment in complete contrast to the lyrics?

There are those moments in songs where what is being said is in complete contrast to what is being heard. In "Everybody Ought to Have a Maid" from *A Funny Thing Happened on the Way to the Forum* by Sondheim, the accompaniment is a happy, jaunty up-tempo song while the lyrics promote female servitude.

That's irony for ya!

4.   How does harmony function in the song?

Harmony is the combination of individual notes played simultaneously, forming chords that underscore the lyric and melody line. Harmonies can be tense or relaxed. More tense harmonies ask for more intense singing. Some chords sound happy. Some chords sound sad. In "Far from the Home I Love" from *Fiddler on the Roof* by Bock and Harnick, as Hodel weighs the pros and cons of moving away from the family, the harmony reflects her inner feelings. It starts out with sad sounding chords (minor key). As she reflects on all the good times the harmony shifts to happy sounding chords (major key). The fluctuation between major and minor mirrors the conflict Hodel feels as she ultimately decides to move away from home.

M — Melody Line

Melody Line is, literally, the shape of a line formed if you connected all the notes of the melody — musical connect the dots! This element helps us discover the melodical, as well as the lyrical, peaks and valleys. As we speak lines in a play, we use vocal inflection to give emphasis to certain words, phrases, and ideas. We naturally utilize pitch in our speaking voice to affect the person to whom we are speaking and get what we need. We also use stressed and unstressed patterns to achieve the same goal. The melody line gives us a road map for where we will use pitch and stress to do so. Most of the time melody lines will follow what the lyric is saying — if the emotional stakes are high the melody line will go up to a high note. If the emotional stakes are lower, the melody line will reflect that.

How do you distinguish the Melody Line in your song?

Ask these questions:

1.   What is the shape of the melody line? Does it go up? Does it go down?

This question is best answered by simply taking a pencil and drawing a line from note to note in your song. Easy! You will notice long curves, short curves, jagged zigzags, straight lines, straight diagonal lines going up and/or down, etc. It is your song's roller coaster ride. After you have done that simple exercise, go on to the following questions.

2.   What lyrics are being sung in connection to the shape of the melody line? Is the lyric a heightened moment? Is it a lessened moment?

Now that you have played musical connect the dots, read the lyrics to find the heightened moments. Go back to the music and see how the melody line and the lyrics align. Most likely the most emotional part lyrically will be at the highest moment musically. Many times composers will use sequences or patterns to get to a high note or to a low note. You can look at this like winding up for a pitch in baseball. As the pitcher swings his arm around he builds momentum to catapult the ball across the plate. Musical sequences and patterns have the same affect — building momentum to catapult us into the peak of emotion lyrically. Towards the end of Pasek and Paul's "Requiem" from *Dear Evan Hanson*, as Zoe purges the pent-up feelings toward her dead brother, her emotional state peaks as the melody line winds up and up to the highest note of the song.

3.   Does the rhythm of the melody line reflect how the lyric would be spoken?

The melody line in "Moments in the Woods" from Sondheim's *Into the Woods* is a perfect example of how pitch and stress aids the delivery of the lyric. As the Baker's Wife asks questions regarding her recent encounter with Cinderella's Prince, the melody is segmented and sequential as an answer is being sought out. Jumps in the melodic line also give importance to certain words. She uses these important words to put into perspective the reasoning behind the encounter.

Answering the questions for each of the members of the T.E.A.M. will allow you to make specific choices that best suit the song.

Chapter 6
Scrimmage

One of the definitions of the word scrimmage from *The Oxford Advanced American Dictionary* is: "A practice game of football, soccer, basketball, etc."

So now's the time to put the analysis into practice.

In the previous two chapters we have walked you through what many would consider text and music analysis (your checklists). The purpose of this is to understand the given circumstances of the play and the character. Now it is our task to take all of those separate data points and assemble them into the physical and emotional environment in which the song takes place. Sanford Meisner described acting as "the ability to behave truthfully under the imaginary circumstances." Having constructed the imaginary circumstances, we are now prepared to ask the question that will make this song yours: "What would I do if I were in this situation?"

The purpose of a scrimmage game is not to win, but rather to evaluate how your own team functions in game-like circumstances. Having assembled the members of our T.E.A.M it is now time to put them into the game!

In order to consolidate this data let us align the T.E.A.M. work with the Ws.

Tonal Color aligns with the Who:

•   18 years of age is different from 48 years of age.

•   A factory worker is different from a corporate CEO.

Energy/Emotion aligns with What #4:

- The reception of shockingly bad news is different from the reception of surprisingly good news.

- The recognition that things cannot continue the way they have, is different from the discovery that nothing will ever be the same.

Accompaniment aligns with Where and When:

- A major urban center is different from a rural environment.

- A sunrise is different from a sunset.

Melody Line aligns with What #2 and #3:

- When stating facts, our inflection remains relatively static. In moments of discovery, our inflection increases in range.

- The high note in the melody line is frequently the "Ah-Ha!" moment in the song.

So now you have begun singing from a personal point of view. Work your way through the song, moment to moment, always remembering what you need. As you discover each lyric in that moment, visualize the images contained in that lyric.

Chapter 7
Play by Play

As we watch any game of sports, the game is broken down in a play-by-play analysis. Each game is composed of individual moments, each preceding moment shapes the moment that comes next. In the previous chapters we provided the ground rules — "checklists" — for how the game is played. Now it's time for us to break down the game moment by moment. This is where we take a deeper dive into the lyrics themselves.

We have encouraged you to always assume that everything in the text is intentional. The author's choices are specific and with purpose. We must now make those words our own. Every sound within a word, every picture painted by the words must be specific and real to us if we are to make it real for others.

According to *Meriam-Webster Dictionary,* onomatopoeia means "the naming of a thing or action by a vocal imitation of the sound associated with it. (such as buzz or hiss)." S.M. Volkonski said in *The Expressive Word,* "If vowels are a river and consonants are the banks, it is necessary to reinforce the later lest there be floods."

Vowels tend to carry the emotion of the song. Consonants shape that emotion into action. The sounds contained in words are capable of evoking emotions within us and others. We argue that there are more words that are onomatopoetic than most of us may think.

How do you discover these?

Ask these questions:

1.   How does the word FEEL in your mouth as you pronounce it?

2.   Does the word contain long, open vowels or short clipped vowels?

3.   Does the word contain consonants that can be held or short percussive consonants?

4.   Does the word sound like what it means?

Here's an exercise: Say the word kiss out loud. Now say the word smooch. While these two words essentially mean the same, they feel different in the mouth. The *k* and *s* sound in kiss are further back in the mouth, the vowel is very short, and the lips are neutral. But when you say the word smooch, the initial consonant places your lips in the position of a kiss. The vowel maintains that lip position. Even the final *ch* sound mimics the sound of the end of a smooch. This is an example of onomatopoeia in action.

Now that we have discussed the feel and sound of the words, let's talk about visual images painted with the words.

Say a song mentions a tree. Does the song specify the type of tree? A willow draws different images than a giant oak. Look at a picture of a willow tree. Now look at a picture of a giant oak. They are both trees but do you get the same feelings as you look at each tree?

What if the song doesn't specify the type of tree? For all the reasons listed above, you must!

Songs are filled with images. While it is tempting for actors to experience these images internally, if we are to affect our partner and get what we need, we must make these images external, vibrant, vigorous, and real. When we sing, we are painting with words. The combination of the literal feel of the word or words as you pronounce them combined with the specific visualization of the word or words is yet another way to make the song yours — personal and specific.

Chapter 8
Game Day!

By this point you have dug deep into the T.E.A.M. process. You have asked and answered the 9 Ws. In the previous chapter you put all of that analysis into practice. And you have practiced the song many times.

So now what?

When we ask our students to come in and share the work they have done, the question they haven't asked out loud is "How do I bring all that analysis and practice into the song in this moment?"

Here's your Game Day checklist:

1.   Have I fully warmed up the part of my voice that will give me the best "T"? (tonal color)

2.   Do I have the "E" (energy/tempo/feel) of the song solidly in my head and body so I can give the best information to the accompanist?

3.   Did I sing through — whether out loud or in my head — the song to bring back to mind the "A" and "M"?

4.   Who am I?

5.   Where am I?

6.   To whom am I speaking?

7.   What do I need?

8.   What just happened that requires me to sing?

If you have successfully answered these questions you are ready to go into the audition room or go on to the stage.

Trust is the next factor. All too often when we walk into the audition room or walk onto the stage our focus shifts to how we are being perceived. When our mind shifts to "How am I doing?" we place less focus onto "What am

I doing?" By keeping the T.E.A.M. process front and center you will keep your mind focused on what you are doing moment to moment. When you focus on the *what*, the *how* takes care of itself. Know that the work you have done is quality and you are in control.

Chapter 9
Postgame Analysis

Once you have sung your song in whatever capacity, you must be able to look back and analyze your success. Keeping an open and objective mind about your performance is what makes us better at our craft.

Going back to Anthony Bourdain, "Practicing your craft in expert fashion is noble, honorable, and satisfying."

So how do we do that?

This time we will ask:

1.   What moments did you feel were most successful? Why?

2.   What moments felt most connected? Why?

3.   In moments that were less successful, can you identify any missing or weak T.E.A.M. elements?

4.   In moments that were less successful, can you identify any missing or weak Ws?

The answers to these questions will lead you back into your analysis and practice.

Outro

This book is a synthesis of the questions and experiences with our students over many combined years. We have attempted to define a concrete process. We are not claiming this is the definitive process. We are claiming that this is a process from which our students have benefitted.

We hope that the process defined in this book will be as useful to you as it has been to our students. If that proves true, we'd love to see ragged copies of this paperback sticking out of coat pockets and dance bags in subways and Ubers around the world or digital versions on your phone!

While our process has been primarily shaped by our experiences with our students, it is also informed by those who preceded us.

Not only the known great teachers we have quoted in this book, but by our colleagues and mentors.

Now it's your turn.

To inspire you on your journey, we offer one of our favorite quotations.

"Talent is an amalgam of high sensitivity; easy vulnerability; high sensory equipment (seeing, hearing, touching, smelling, tasting — intensely); a vivid imagination as well as a grip on reality; the desire to communicate one's own experience and sensations, to make one's self heard and seen. Talent alone is not enough. Character and ethics, a point of view about the world in which you live, and an education, can and must be acquired and developed." — Uta Hagen *Respect for Acting*

About the Authors

Lisa Campbell Albert

Originally from Belleville, Illinois, Lisa received her Bachelor of Music from Southern Illinois University in Edwardsville, IL and her Master of Music from Webster University in St. Louis, Missouri. Presently, Lisa serves as an Adjunct Associate Professor on the faculty of the Sargent Conservatory of Theatre Arts at Webster University where she teaches song analysis and vocal coaching. Previously, she resided on faculty in both the Arts Department and Music Department at Washington University in St. Louis, Missouri, where she received the ArtSci Council Faculty Award for Excellence in Teaching. Lisa served as Music Supervisor/Music Director at STAGES ST. LOUIS from 2008-2020. Lisa is the recipient of the Kevin Kline Award for Outstanding Musical Direction (2011) and the annual Broadway World STL Award for Outstanding Musical Direction (2014-2018). Lisa is a coach to singers in St. Louis, New York City, as well as nationally. Lisa continues to play music with her husband, Tim Albert, in the St. Louis based blues band Uncle Albert.

Bill Lynch

Originally from Seaford, Long Island, NY, Bill received his Bachelor of Arts in Theatre from University of Maryland, College Park campus and his Master of Fine Arts in Acting from Florida State University/Asolo Conservatory for Actor Training in Sarasota, FLA. Recently, Bill retired as Professor Emeritus from the faculty of the Sargent Conservatory of Theatre Arts at Webster University. During his tenure, Bill taught acting, text analysis, vocal production, speech/dialects, and song study. Bill is a recipient of the William T. Kemper Award for Excellence in Teaching. Bill joined Actors' Equity Association in 1989 and has performed in over 100 productions ranging from Shakespeare to Simon to Sondheim. In addition, he has served as vocal/dialect coach for over 50 productions.

HISTRIA

BOOKS

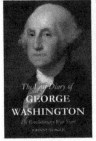